EARTHY HOMEMAKER'S COOKBOOK

Simple Recipes and Useful Tips

Freda Maxfield

Copyright © 2022 Freda Maxfield

All rights reserved

No part of this book may be reproduced, or stored in a retrieval system, or transmitted in any form or by any means, electronic, mechanical, photocopying, recording, or otherwise, without express written permission of the publisher.

Illustrations by Freda Maxfield

Grateful thanks to the readers of my blog who asked me to compile my recipes in a book. A huge thank you to my wonderful daughter, Samantha, for her unfailing encouragement and technical assistance. Also to my husband, Allan, for his love and appreciation of the things I do. Many thanks also to my son, Jason, and my sister, Mavis, for their support and patient listening whenever I mentioned this project.

CONTENTS

Title Page
Copyright
Dedication
INTRODUCTION — 1
OVEN SETTINGS CONVERSION TABLE — 3
USEFUL TIPS — 4
ONE-PAN MEALS — 12
MEAT MEALS — 21
VEGETARIAN MEALS — 27
CHEESE DISHES — 35
SANDWICHES — 44
SOUPS — 48
CAKES AND PIES — 54
PUDDINGS — 75
SAUCES — 88
PRESERVING — 96
About The Author — 113

INTRODUCTION

Food is not just an essential to sustaining life. It's a sensual experience. The anticipation, the taste, aroma and look of food should be life's great pleasures. Likewise the making of food should delight and satisfy. The scent of baking in a warm kitchen on a wet day, the glowing colour of homemade jam spread on toast, a cupboard full of tasty chutney to spice up a stodgy winter meal. All these and more should be enjoyed and contribute to a life full of homely comforts.

This cookbook arose from the blog I write about homecrafts such as gardening, cooking, baking and preserving. All the recipes are my own and have found favour with many of my readers. Consequently, I was asked to put them together in book form to make them accessible as a collection.

Like me, you've probably bought countless cookbooks which had instant appeal, only to find later that you had little use for them. Often too sophisticated for general use or full of obscure ingredients which you never use again.

I grew tired of recipes that didn't work, were too complicated to bother with or required silly ingredients, so for years I have invented my own with pleasing results. Everything here is easy to do, full of nutrition and tastes really good. Otherwise I wouldn't offer them to anyone else. As I say in the introduction to my blog "I'm not going to make you say, "Oh, that's too complicated" or "I couldn't do that!"

These are simple, delicious recipes for practical cooks with a taste for good food, not concocted in a television kitchen or a food manufacturer's laboratory. I've tried and tested every one in my own kitchen with everyday ingredients.

Some recipes need specific weights and measures, others are adaptable for your own needs or tastes. This is clearly stated along with step by step instructions.

I mostly work with small quantities but these can be increased easily to provide larger meals.

For more about my cooking, gardening, poetry, paintings and crafts, illustrated with my own photographs, take a look at my blog. Readers tell me they find it inspirational, soothing and useful. I hope you will too. You will find it by clicking the link below. www.earthyhomemakernet.wordpress.com

OVEN SETTINGS CONVERSION TABLE

I use an electric fan oven. Many of you will use gas so I include here a conversion table to show the equivalent settings.

Degrees centigrade	Gas
140	1
150	2
160	3
180	4
190	5
200	6
220	7
230	8
240	9

USEFUL TIPS

Even if you enjoy cooking as I do, it's good to know some quick methods and essential equipment to make life easier. Although cooking, baking and preserving are satisfying pursuits, let's face it, they are also tiring. There are ways to make the kitchen a happy environment.

You may want to try the recipes right away but here are some useful tips to save you time and energy when you cook. If you want to read them later, that's fine. I will add useful tips to recipes along the way.

Invest in some good modern equipment and utensils.

FOOD PROCESSOR

A food processor is an essential tool. It's not just about speed. You can make cheap and satisfying dishes that would either be impossible or take hours to do without one.

Even by only using the basic blade you can reduce ingredients to fine crumbs, combine them to make them workable or liquidise them.

If you need a cake mixing quickly or a stuffing for mushrooms, onions chopping extremely finely without teary, stinging eyes or bananas blended to add to a pudding, a food processor makes light work of them all.

It doesn't need to be top of the range with every imaginable gadget. However, a mill is very useful if you need to grind nuts finely and a blending jug is good if you make a lot of soups. I find

I don't use the slicing and grating accessories but you may find these useful.

If you find you have stale bread, don't ever throw it away (unless it's mouldy, of course). Make breadcrumbs in the processor and freeze them for lots of dishes. More about this later.

I use breadcrumbs in many of my recipes.

MICROWAVE OVEN

This is not essential but certainly makes life easier. I use mine for softening onions before putting them into savoury bakes, gently cooking sliced courgettes, thawing bread or cakes when necessary and cooking lentils. I also have a very good recipe for peanut sauce cooked in the microwave oven.

They have many uses for cooking whole dishes or for making sauces but you will not find me recommending them for ready-meals bought from the supermarket. The aim here is to assist in the cooking of home-made meals.

ELECTRIC MIXER

A small hand mixer with beaters is a good aid to mixing cakes. A wooden spoon will do it but needs a strong hand to mix thoroughly, especially when adding all ingredients together. They usually have several speeds but even a cheap one with only one will do the job.

HAND BLENDER

Very useful for soups, especially if you only want to thicken but not liquidise. Good for smoothies too. Best used in a deep bowl or pan as they can be very splashy! Because of this, always allow hot liquids to cool slightly before blending.

THERMAL COOKER

This is just a large thermal flask with a pan inside. Mine is Mr D's eco-friendly thermal cooker, bought online. It was expensive but worth its weight in gold. Joints of meat, chickens, rice puddings, stews and soups can be cooked in this without power. Takes a few minutes on the hob to start the cooking. The cooking pan is then placed snugly inside the thermal flask and left for the required time. The heat is retained and it continues to cook the food. It's a brilliant piece of equipment and repays the initial expense. Great for the budget and very ecologically sound.

I was at first sceptical that meat cooked in a lot of water instead of roasting would be tasty. I was worrying needlessly. I have cooked chicken, lamb, turkey breast and beef in it and they were tender and full of flavour. Plus there is delicious stock afterwards to use with leftover scraps for soups.

If you like rice pudding but hate the skin, the thermal cooker is ideal. It makes a lovely skinless pudding.

WEIGHTS AND MEASURES

A good set of scales with both metric and imperial measures is an absolutely essential item. Try to find one with the weights divided into the smallest quantities, ie. grams and ounces. The bowl, ideally, should have a pouring lip. Round bowls look attractive but don't tip the contents cleanly into the mixing bowl.

A set of cup measures is really useful. They can be an easy way to measure small amounts. Choose ones with clear markings and a clean construction to make washing easy.

A silicon mat for pastry with cake tin sizes marked on it is helpful. Sometimes recipes will require a certain size of cake tin. Not all cake tins are marked with their measurement but the mat will quickly show you the size. Also saves wear and tear on the worktop when cutting pastry shapes and is easy to wash and dry afterwards.

COOKING KNIVES

Small paring knives, a peeling tool and a chef's knife are essential equipment. The chef's knife is best if it is self-sharpening. These come with a sheath which grinds the knife each time it's pushed back into place.

KITCHEN SCISSORS

A couple of pairs of sharp small scissors are invaluable for snipping herbs, the stems from kale or trimming bacon. They must be washable. Keep a separate pair for non-food jobs.

CAKE LINERS

Liners for cake tins are available in different shapes and sizes. These save greasing the cake tin and keep it clean during baking. They make washing the tins easy.

Note: Bun tins are horrible to wash and paper cake cases are difficult to fill without slopping cake mixture over the tins. I discovered that it's much easier to bake small individual cakes in a large roasting tin. The cake mixture is poured in, baked and cut into squares once cooled.
See my SWEET-TREAT SQUARES section.

CAKE SPATULAS

A flexible silicone spatula will scrape all the cake mixture from a mixing bowl.
A stainless steel icing spatula is also useful for lifting cakes divided into squares and for sliding under sponges to remove from the base of the baking tin.

SALT

Salt is not just a condiment and flavouring for cooking. It is useful in other ways.
When slicing peeled apples and pears there is no need to have a lemon handy to stop them from going brown. Just put about a

tablespoon of table salt into half a litre of water and place the slices into this. Swish them about to coat the surfaces. Rinse and drain when ready to use in your recipe. They will not taste salty once they're rinsed. Cheaper, more convenient and more effective than lemon juice.

When preserving vegetables it's better to use sea salt. This has no additives and draws out any excess moisture from the vegetables before pickling or making into chutney.

PRESERVING EQUIPMENT

If you want to preserve fruit and vegetables it's best to have a few essential tools to hand.

One thing you'll definitely need is a large stockpot with a lid. This will hold a substantial amount of chutney or jam. A stainless steel one is best. Never buy an old-fashioned brass preserving pan. The metal is toxic and will react with vinegar.

A large bowl or two will be needed for salting vegetables prior to cooking chutney or pickles. I have two large but lightweight stainless steel ones which double up as baking bowls.

A funnel with a wide mouth but small enough to fit inside the top of jam jars keeps jars clean when filling them. Stainless steel is better than plastic for this as it's best to fill jars with very hot jam or chutney in order to seal them.

A soup ladle helps to transfer chutney or jam into the jars.

A wooden spoon with an extra-long handle is a big help for jam making. It will prevent the bubbling jam from splashing on your arms or hands (extremely painful!)

STALE BREAD

Dry bread loses its appeal for sandwiches but has many good uses.

Breadcrumbs are easy to make in a food processor, freeze well, and are very versatile. They make excellent toppings for savoury bakes, stuffing for mushrooms or courgettes, adding to meatballs or vegetarian sausages.

Bread pieces make wonderful puddings soaked with an egg custard and with additions such as fruit or savoury ingredients.

Dry bread, cut into cubes and added to basil, olives, tomatoes, garlic and olive oil makes a delicious salad.

When fried gently in a little olive oil, bread cubes or pieces make an excellent omelette. The bread should be gently fried then the beaten egg poured over and allowed to set.

FREEZING

If you grow vegetables and fruit you may find you have a surplus. Freezing them is simple. The stockpot mentioned above for jam making is also useful for freezing.

Vegetables need to be as fresh as possible and prepared while water is coming to a boil. They need to be boiled for a few minutes, then drained and quickly cooled in very cold water.

Lots of books are available with appropriate times for blanching different vegetables. If you intend to do much freezing it's a good idea to invest in a good guide.

I used to freeze in polythene bags but now I'm aware of how bad these are, I use reusable containers. I save ice-cream tubs for this purpose.

Fruit doesn't need to be blanched. Soft fruits and rhubarb are best for freezing.

Strawberries freeze well but are a little disappointing when thawed. They are perfect for jam making though and I also cook them gently and add sugar, allow to cool and eat with yoghurt or ice cream. Really delicious.

Raspberries thaw well and blueberries are very good. Blueberries thawed in a sieve over a bowl produce a fabulous juice.

Apple slices will freeze but turn brown very quickly when thawed. Better to cook them into applesauce first and allow to cool. This way they keep their colour and are ready to fill pies, or to eat as they are, once thawed.

ONE-PAN MEALS

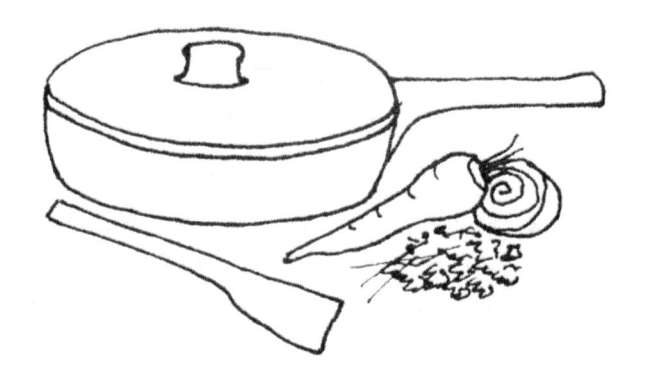

ONE-PAN MEALS

This method of cooking is not only easy but retains nutrients and flavour. It saves on dishwashing and uses little fuel. What's not to like?

You will need a deep frying pan with a lid. A heavy based pan is best.

I have a basic formula which works for a variety of ingredients. Quantities are dependent on your needs but this basic method stays the same.

Always begin with a small amount of water – just enough to come halfway up the vegetables you will be adding or less if adding cooked rice. Stir a good stock cube into this. Usually a vegetable stock cube is all you will need but sometimes a meat one is needed.

I use microwave rice which is pre-cooked but I don't heat it in the microwave. It's ideal for tipping into these one-pan meals. The rice absorbs the stock, flavours and vitamins. Far easier than boiling it separately. Produces a tasty and quick version of risotto.

FISH AND RICE

Kallo organic Vegetable Stock Cube
Frozen Fish fillets
Frozen cooked Rice
Small clove of Garlic or small sliced Onion
Vegetables, eg. a selection of the following: Peas, Sweetcorn, Green Beans, Carrots
(These can be fresh or frozen.)
Creme fraiche.

Prepare any fresh vegetables and slice or chop.
If using onion, slice and cook for a few minutes in a little heated oil until semi-transparent. Don't allow them to burn. Then add the water and other ingredients as follows.
Put a small amount of water in the pan. Just enough to cook the ingredients but to leave a fairly dry pan at the end of cooking. When it's hot, crumble a vegetable stock cube in and stir to dissolve.
Add the vegetables.
Bring to a boil and stir in frozen rice.
Place fish fillets on top of vegetables and rice.
Make sure it comes back to the boil before turning the heat down to a simmer. Put the lid on the pan and time for 10-15 minutes depending on how well you want the vegetables cooked.
Check occasionally that the pan is not dry and food sticking. Add a drop of water if necessary.
Check that the vegetables are tender. If they're ready, remove the pan from the heat and stir in a spoonful of crème fraiche.
No need to remove the fish if you stir gently but if the pan is too crowded place the fish on a plate, stir in crème fraiche then replace the fish to warm through and serve.

This can also be done with potatoes or sweet potatoes instead of rice.

For potatoes, peel and cut into small chunks. Have a little more water in the pan but not too much - just about halfway up the vegetables. Add potatoes to the pan with vegetables and cook until tender. If you prefer not to use crème fraiche, mix a little cornflour to a smooth runny paste with a little water and stir into the stock at the end. The vegetable stock cube and juices make a flavourful sauce.

For sweet potatoes, peel and slice into chunks, add with vegetables and cook until tender. They cook quickly so best to choose vegetables which cook in the same amount of time – about ten minutes. Either stir in crème fraiche or thicken the stock as given above.

FREDA MAXFIELD

LEMON HADDOCK IN A CREAMY SAUCE

Vegetable Stock Cube
1 medium Leek
Celeriac
Carrots
Frozen Peas
Frozen pre-cooked Rice
Frozen Haddock Fillets
1 Lemon
Half fat Creme fraiche

Prepare the leek and slice thinly.
Prepare the celeriac and cut into small pieces.
Peel and slice carrots.
Put a small amount of water into a frying pan and heat.
Stir in a crumbled stock cube.
Add vegetables and rice. Put the lid on the pan.
Bring to the boil then turn heat to low and simmer for 5 or 6 minutes.
Place fish fillets on top of vegetables and rice. Bring to the boil then reduce heat.
Put the lid back on and cook for 10 minutes more.
When the vegetables and fish are tender, gently stir in a good spoonful of creme fraiche.
Serve immediately.

CHICKEN AND RICE WITH GINGER

Kallo organic Chicken Stock Cube
Chicken breasts, cut into pieces or Goujons
Clove of Garlic
Frozen cooked rice
Tin of Green Giant organic Sweetcorn
Green Beans, fresh or frozen
2 or 3 lumps of Stem Ginger   (see recipe in PRESERVING)

Put a small amount of water into a deep frying pan with a lid. The water needs to reduce until almost dry at the end, so don't add a lot. You can top it up a little if necessary during cooking.

Bring to a boil and stir in a chicken stock cube. Add chicken, vegetables, crushed garlic and rice. Bring back to boil and stir to mix ingredients, then turn down to simmer. Chop ginger into small lumps and stir in.

Cook for 15 minutes with the lid on. Check to see if it's becoming too dry and sticking. If so, add a few drops of water.

Serve when everything is cooked sufficiently.

CHICKEN AND SWEET POTATOES IN CREAMY SAUCE

This is such an easy meal and really delicious. I haven't specified quantities as it's not necessary. You can use as much or as little of the ingredients as you like. It's the combination of flavours and the creamy sauce which make this special.

Cooked Chicken breast
Garlic
Chicken Stock Cube
Carrots
Sweet Potatoes
Frozen Peas
Creme fraiche or half-fat Creme fraiche

Peel carrots and sweet potatoes. Slice carrots thinly. Slice sweet potatoes into thick slices.
Put a small amount of water into a deep frying pan.
Add the crumbled stock cube and crushed garlic. Stir.
Add carrots, sweet potatoes and peas.
Cut cooked chicken into small chunks and add to the pan.
Bring to the boil and stir to distribute ingredients, then lower heat and put the lid on the pan.
Simmer for 15 minutes or until vegetables are tender and chicken well heated.
When ready, stir in 2 tablespoons of creme fraiche and serve.

If you want to make it a bit fancier, a few basil leaves sprinkled on top look colourful and go well with the flavours.

TURKEY AND CRANBERRY SPECIAL

1 Kallo organic Chicken Stock Cube
Cooked Turkey pieces
Sliced Onion
Olive Oil
Small Brussells Sprouts or Green Beans
Carrots
Dried sweetened Cranberries (Whitworths or Ocean Spray)
Frozen cooked Rice

Prepare vegetables: peel and slice carrots thinly, trim sprouts or use frozen button sprouts or green beans chopped into short lengths..

Heat a tablespoon of olive oil to medium heat in a deep frying pan and fry the onion gently until transparent. Don't allow it to brown.

Take off the heat and add a little water, just enough to cover the pan. Bring to boil and stir in the stock cube.

Add vegetables, turkey, rice and cranberries. If necessary add a little more water but only enough to keep it moist.

Bring to boil then turn down to a simmer. Put the lid on the pan and cook for 15 minutes.

Check part way through that the pan is not going dry. Add a few drops if necessary. Make sure the temperature is maintained.

When vegetables are tender it's ready to serve.

FREDA MAXFIELD

LAMB CUTLETS WITH POTATOES AND GRAVY

Don't use cutlets with splinters of bone because these will be retained in the gravy.
Makes enough for two.

2 Lamb cutlets (Trim fat or brown in a little oil first)
1 Oxo cube
Potatoes, cut into small chunks
Carrots, sliced
Frozen Peas
Garlic
A little red wine (optional)
Cornflour

If you want tender meat, cook the cutlets for an hour in the pan before adding vegetables.
Heat a little oil and fry the cutlets for a few minutes if necessary.
If the preliminary browning isn't required, put a little water in the pan, sufficient to cover the cutlets. Stir in the crumbled oxo cube, crushed garlic and red wine if using. Bring to boil. Place the cutlets in the pan and put the lid on. Turn down to a simmer.
If tender meat is required, leave the meat to cook with the lid on the pan until the desired tenderness is achieved. Test for tenderness then proceed.
Add vegetables. Replace the lid, bring back to simmer and leave to cook for 12 – 15 minutes until tender.
Mix a spoonful of cornflour to a smooth runny paste with a little water. Pour into the hot stock while stirring to thicken. If the pan is too crowded remove the meat while you thicken the stock and replace it in the gravy for a few minutes to reheat.

Retains all the taste and nourishment and tastes really good. Only one pan to wash and little fuel used.

MEAT MEALS

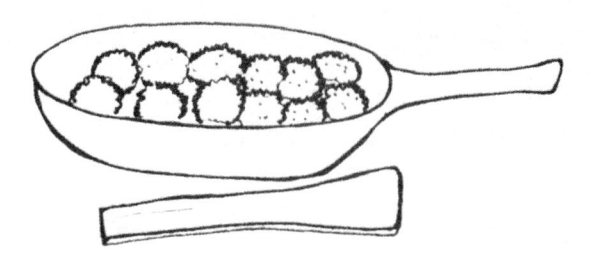

MEAT MEALS

CHICKEN

CHICKEN AND BACON ROLLS

Chicken breasts per person
Streaky Bacon

Heat oven to 190C/170C fan oven
Slice the chicken into long thick strips.
Flatten slightly and place a strip of bacon on each piece and roll up with bacon on the outside.
Place the rolls close together in a greased roasting tin or baking dish. Add a couple of spoonfuls of water to the dish. Cover with foil and cook for 1 hour.
Remove foil and put back into the oven to crisp the bacon, about 20 minutes.
Will keep warm under a piece of foil until ready to serve.

These are really tender and go well with my PEANUT SAUCE, recipe in SAUCES section, or crème fraiche.

CHICKEN AND GINGER SAVOURY CAKES

This is good when you have a bit of cooked leftover chicken. It's moist and tasty and so easy to make. Dried herbs are fine but don't overdo the amount or the chicken taste will be overpowered.

Cooked Chicken breast
1 lump of Stem Ginger
1 small Onion, sliced
Herbs eg. Marjoram and Parsley
Salt and Pepper

Whiz all together in a food processor.
Form into flattened cakes. Brown in a little hot oil in a frying pan.

VARIATION WITH ABOVE INGREDIENTS
The ingredients for the chicken and ginger cakes, without the additional cooking, make a good sandwich filling. Go easy on the onion and herbs and combine well in the food processor. Spread on bread.

CHICKEN AND RICE SALAD

Another suggestion for cooked chicken leftovers.

Cooked Chicken breast, chopped
Balsamic Vinegar
Soy Sauce
Ginger Syrup
Cooked Rice
Cooked Sweetcorn
Basil leaves
Green Beans, lightly cooked.
1 small Onion, thinly sliced
Salt and Pepper

Combine vinegar, soy sauce and syrup in equal amounts in a bowl and toss the pieces of chicken in it. Leave for a few minutes for flavours to penetrate the chicken.
Meanwhile prepare the salad. Cook beans.
Put cooked rice, sweetcorn, thinly sliced onion, beans, salt and pepper and torn basil leaves into a bowl.
Add chicken and toss well to combine.

TURKEY

Also see my ONE-PAN MEALS section.

TURKEY BURGERS
Makes 4 or 5

454g Turkey Mince
1 large Egg
1 Apple
1 Garlic clove or 1 small Onion
Salt and Pepper

Heat the oven to 200C/180C fan oven.

Peel, core and chop the apple into small pieces.
Crush the garlic or if using onion, chop the onion finely.
Add the apple, garlic or onion, egg, salt and pepper to the mince and mix well with a fork or clean hands.
When well combined, form into flat burgers. Makes four or five.
Place burgers in a greased roasting tin and cover the tin with foil.
Cook for 30 minutes.
Uncover and cook uncovered for another ten to fifteen minutes.

It's a good idea to roast squash or parsnips at the same time. These go well with the burgers and it makes good use of the oven.

PORK

SAUSAGEMEAT BALLS

These make an economical and tasty meal which are sensational with my PEANUT SAUCE and rice, see recipe in SAUCES section. If you can't find sausagemeat with added ingredients, chop a small onion very finely and add to the meat with a pinch of dried herbs or finely chopped fresh ones.

Makes 12 balls

350g Pork Sausagemeat with added Onion and Herbs
50g Breadcrumbs
1 large Egg
Vegetable Stock Cube

Combine the ingredients with a fork or with clean hands.
Form into twelve balls and put into the fridge for about 20 minutes to firm up.
Heat a little oil in a deep frying pan.
Brown the balls all over, moving them gently to keep their shape.
When they have browned a little add some water to the pan and add the crumbled vegetable stock cube. Stir gently to distribute the stock.
Turn heat to medium and simmer the balls for about 15-20 minutes.
Lift out with a slotted spoon and discard stock.

They are a bit fragile at the browning stage but keep their shape well once the simmering begins.

Serve with my Peanut Sauce and rice for a special meal or with baked beans for an everyday meal.

Any leftover balls are good broken up and added to an omelette.

VEGETARIAN MEALS

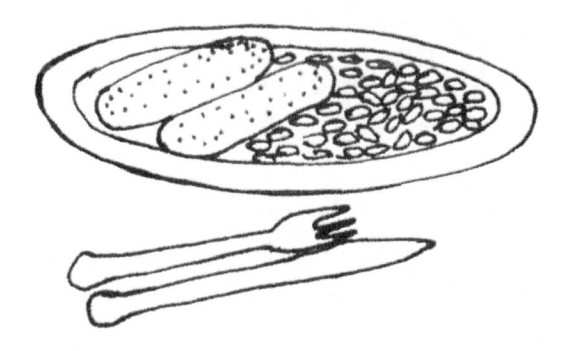

VEGETARIAN MEALS

I find cashew nuts very useful in so many of my recipes. They provide protein and when they're ground they give a creamy texture. The taste is subtle and mild which makes it ideal for sweet or savoury dishes.

NUTTY SAUSAGES

For these I use small bunches of fresh herbs such as parsley with marjoram, basil with marjoram or parsley with sage. Just use a mixture of your favourites or whatever is available. I haven't tried them with dried herbs although I'm sure it would work. If you only have dry herbs available only use a very small amount or they will taste too strong.

50g Cashew Nuts
75g Bread
1 small Onion
1 Apple
Pinches of Fresh Herbs, a selection according to preference
1 large Egg
Salt and Pepper
Plain Flour

Grind the nuts in a food processor. Add the bread broken into small pieces.
Slice the onion into the food processor bowl.
Peel and core the apple and slice into the bowl.
Add the washed herbs (discard any hard stalks), salt and pepper.
Process to combine and chop ingredients finely.
Add the egg and whiz again to mix it in.
Put the flour on a plate and add a little salt and pepper.
With floured hands remove a quantity of the sausage mixture (makes four) and form a sausage shape. Roll the sausage in the flour and place on another plate. Repeat with the rest.
Place the sausages in the fridge for 15 – 30 minutes to firm up.
Heat some oil in a frying pan to sizzling temperature. Slide the sausages in.
Turn down the heat and brown all sides, turning them as necessary until done.
Serve with your favourite vegetables.

Good with tomato ketchup or chutney.

CASHEW CAKES

250ml Milk (Oat milk or dairy)
1 quarter cup of Cornflour
Garlic clove
Finely chopped Small Onion
50g Cashew Nuts
100g Breadcrumbs
Half a cup of Sweetcorn, tinned or frozen
Salt and Pepper
A little Plain Flour

Crush the garlic clove. Heat the milk with the garlic and onion.
While milk is coming to boil, mix the cornflour with an extra drop of milk to a smooth runny paste.
Stir cornflour into boiling milk, stirring while you pour. It will become quite thick.
Remove from heat.
Grind the nuts in a food processor or mill.
Add nuts, breadcrumbs, sweetcorn, salt and pepper to the thickened sauce and mix well.
Allow to cool completely so that it will set.
Put the flour onto a plate with a little salt and pepper. With floured hands scoop out small portions of the mixture and form into flat cakes.
Heat a little oil in a frying pan to sizzling point. Place the cakes in the pan and turn the heat down a bit. Brown both sides.

Add a little chilli powder while mixing if you prefer a spicier recipe.

CREAMY PARSNIP FLAN

Pastry for a flan dish approximately 8 inches/22.5cm in diameter (See my PASTRY section or use your favourite recipe)

Approx 500g Parsnips
80g Cashews
1 small Onion
1 Vegetable Stock Cube
1 large Egg
half – to a whole small red Chilli
Salt and Pepper
2 heaped tablespoons Creme fraiche

Make pastry, line the greased dish and chill in the fridge.
Prepare parsnips. Wash, peel and slice. Cook in a little water for 10 minutes.
While the parsnips cook, grind the nuts in a food processor.
Drain the parsnips and allow to cool slightly.
Heat oven to 190C/170 fan oven
Slice onion and add with parsnips, crumbled stock cube, salt and pepper, the egg and crème fraiche to the nuts in the food processor. Whiz until well combined.
Chop chilli finely. Amount of this depends on your taste for chilli.
Add the chopped chilli to the mixture and combine briefly.
Put the mixture into the pastry case and spread evenly.
Bake for 40 minutes.

Good hot with vegetables of your choice or cold with pickles or chutney.

COURGETTE FLAN

Pastry for a flan dish approximately 8 inches/22.5cm in diameter. (See my PASTRY section or use your favourite pastry recipe.)

50g Cashew Nuts
2 medium Leeks
1 Courgette
Carton of Oatley Cream
Small red Chilli (optional)
1 large Egg
half a tin of Sweetcorn
Salt and Pepper
A little oil

Prepare pastry and line the greased flan dish. Put into the fridge to chill while making the filling.
Grind the cashews finely.
Prepare and chop leeks. Put into a microwaveable bowl. Soften in the microwave in a splash of olive or sunflower oil for 3 minutes. (Alternatively, cook gently in a frying pan. Don't allow the leeks to brown.)
Heat the oven to 190C/170C fan oven.
Add nuts, chopped chilli,(if using), sweetcorn, salt and pepper and two thirds of the oat cream to the leeks.
Beat the egg, then add and stir to combine.
Put the filling into the pastry case and arrange thin slices of courgette on top.
Brush a little olive oil onto the slices or a few dabs of butter.
Bake for 35 minutes or until filling is set and courgettes tender.

Good with mashed carrots and parsnips.

STUFFED MUSHROOMS

This recipe is enough for two but it's simple to increase quantities for more servings.

2 Large flat Mushrooms
50g Cashew Nuts
50g Breadcrumbs
Half a small Onion
Basil Leaves, small bunch
Salt and Pepper

Cauliflower
Tomatoes
Milk
Creme fraiche

Grind the cashews in a food processor. Add breadcrumbs.
Wash and peel the mushrooms. Carefully scoop out the inside flesh of each mushroom and add the bits to the processor. Place the scooped-out mushrooms in a baking dish.
Heat the oven to 200C/180C fan oven.
Slice the onion into the processor.
Wash and shake the basil leaves and add with salt and pepper.
Whiz to combine well.
Fill the mushrooms with the mixture.
Arrange cauliflower florets and halved tomatoes around the mushrooms and add a few spoonfuls of creme fraiche and milk around the sides. Sprinkle with salt and pepper and stir a little to mix. This makes a lovely sauce.
Bake for 35 minutes.

PEANUT BUTTER LOAF

Peanuts are another good source of protein (unless you're allergic to them, of course.)

4 generous tablespoons Peanut Butter (smooth or chunky)
1 Onion
1 clove of Garlic
1 Lemon
Tin of Baked Beans
100g Breadcrumbs or small pieces of Bread
Small bunch of Parsley
Chilli powder 1- 2 level teaspoons according to taste
Salt and Pepper

Squeeze the lemon. Wash parsley, remove stalks and pat dry. Slice onion.
Heat the oven to 190C/170C fan oven.
Put all ingredients into a food processor and whiz until well mixed.
Put into a loaf tin lined with a cake liner. Cover with foil.
Bake for 1 hour.
Important note: Allow to cool completely before turning out. This allows it to set.

Very good cold but slices can be reheated briefly in a microwave oven.

CHEESE DISHES

CHEESE DISHES

Many recipes call for Italian cheeses. While these are flavoursome I think Britain has wonderful cheeses and perhaps they are overlooked. I love Lancashire for cooking, Cheddar is wonderful for sandwiches and salads and blue cheeses are excellent with crackers.

Here are some everyday dishes which are tasty, satisfying and easy to do.

CHEESEY POTATOES WITH KALE OR CABBAGE

Easiest if a steamer is used but the potatoes and kale or cabbage can, of course, be cooked separately.

Lancashire or Cheddar Cheese
Potatoes
Kale or Cabbage
1 large Onion
Salt and Pepper
Creme fraiche or Soured Cream (optional)

Peel the potatoes, cut into chunks and place in the bottom pan of a steamer. Cover with water.
Wash and trim the kale or cabbage and place in the perforated upper section of the steamer.
Place the kale or cabbage pan over the potato pan.
Bring water to the boil, turn down to medium and cook the vegetables until the potatoes are tender. About 18-20 minutes.
While the vegetables cook, slice the onion and put into a baking dish. Sprinkle with a little olive oil and soften the onion in the microwave for two or three minutes. Don't allow it to brown.
Heat the oven to 200C/180C fan oven.
Grate the cheese if using Cheddar, crumble it if using Lancashire.
When vegetables are ready remove the top pan and put aside.
Drain and mash the potatoes. Add salt and pepper.
Mash the cheese into the potatoes with a fork. Add a couple of spoonfuls of crème fraiche if available.
Place the kale or cabbage over the onions in the dish. Spread the mash over the kale or cabbage.

Bake for 35 - 40 minutes or until golden brown on top.

Cheering winter dish. Good with tomato ketchup or chutney.

FREDA MAXFIELD

BEST EVER CHEESE ON TOAST

Lancashire cheese is superb for toasting. It doesn't become stringy or greasy. It has a fresh, sharp taste and is wonderful with tomatoes.

Sliced White Bloomer Loaf
Lancashire Cheese
Ripe Tomatoes

Heat the grill to maximum.
Toast one side of the bread slices.
Remove the pan from the grill. Using oven gloves, lower the grill shelf.
Turn the bread over and arrange cheese on top. The cheese will crumble so it needs a bit of care.
Place back under the grill and cook until bubbling and becoming golden brown.
While it cooks, slice tomatoes onto plates.
Slide the toasted cheese slices onto the plates using a flat spatula and serve immediately.

CHEESE AND ONION SPECIAL

Precise quantities are not given here because it depends on how much you need to make. It's a see-how-you-go type of recipe but foolproof.

Lancashire or Cheshire Cheese
Onions
Milk
Plain Flour
Olive Oil
Salt and Pepper
Bread

Slice onions thinly. Heat a little olive oil (1 – 2 tablespoons).
Cook the onions on a low heat until they become transparent and soft. Don't allow them to brown.
When onions are soft, stir in a heaped tablespoon of flour to form a paste then add the milk a little at a time while stirring until a smooth sauce forms. Add salt and pepper.
Crumble the cheese and add to the pan. Stir a little while the cheese melts.
Serve with slices of bread.
Vegetables may be served with it to make it more nutritious but very good as it is.

CHEESE AND TOMATOES

My mother used to make this cheap, nutritious and easy meal when I was growing up. She used Cheshire cheese and bought over-ripe tomatoes at a discounted price from the grocer. You don't usually see those now but if you grow your own this is a delicious way to use them. I prefer Lancashire cheese for my version. I think this tastes even better cooked in a cast-iron frying pan.

Lancashire Cheese
Tomatoes
Olive Oil
Salt and Pepper
Bread

Wash and dry the tomatoes. Slice, or if using baby plum tomatoes, halve them.
Heat a small amount of olive oil in a frying pan and add tomatoes. Cook until soft, adding a little water as the juice thickens. (If using a cast-iron pan don't add very cold water. Use slightly warm water or you might crack the pan).
When tomatoes are soft, crumble cheese and add to the pan.
Stir to mix a little while the cheese melts.
Serve with sliced bread and a sprinkle of salt and pepper.

SAVOURY BAKE

Good for using up dry bread and leftover cheese.

Cheddar Cheese
Bread
Onions
Tomatoes
Courgettes.
Basil or Parsley if available

Slice onions thinly and place in a baking dish. Sprinkle a little olive oil over and stir around to coat.
Cook in the microwave for two minutes. Alternatively, cook gently in a frying pan, then put into the baking dish.
Heat oven to 200C/180C fan oven.
Wash herbs and chop. Sprinkle over the onions.
Slice tomatoes and put a layer on top of onions. Do the same with courgettes.
Sprinkle salt and pepper over them.
Bake for 25 minutes.
While the vegs are baking pulse bread pieces and cheese in a food processor to make cheesey
crumbs. Alternatively, break bread into small pieces and mix with grated cheese.
Remove the baking dish from the oven and cover the vegetables with the cheesey crumbs.
Bake again for about 15 – 20 minutes or until the topping is golden brown.

This is also good if you have any leftover cooked vegetables to use such as carrots or kale. Use these instead of the courgettes but put the tomatoes on top of them. Bake as above then cover with crumbs and finish in the same way.

PESTO

This is my version of pesto using cashew nuts instead of pine nuts and Lancashire cheese. I don't recommend Cheddar for this as it is too greasy. Precise quantities are not given but use less nuts than cheese. Taste as you go in order to achieve the mix you want.

Cashew Nuts
Lancashire Cheese
Garlic
Basil leaves
Olive Oil
Salt and Pepper

Put the nuts into a food processor and grind them. Add crumbled cheese and crushed garlic (amount depends on your taste for garlic). Add salt and pepper.
Wash basil leaves and pat dry with kitchen paper. Add to other ingredients.
Whiz to combine well then add olive oil a little at a time.
Whiz until a smooth thick consistency is formed.

Freezes really well in small containers.
Good on pasta, baked potatoes or on crackers.

ITALIAN STYLE SALAD WITH CHEESE

Another good way of using dry bread.

White Bloomer Bread
Baby Plum Tomatoes
Basil leaves
Black Olives
Garlic
Olive Oil
Salt and Pepper
Cheddar Cheese

Cut bread into cubes.
Crush a little garlic clove or part of one.
Put two tablespoons of olive oil with salt and pepper in a serving bowl and add the garlic. Mix.
Add the bread, stirring it about to coat the cubes.
Add halved tomatoes.
Wash and pat dry basil leaves. Tear the leaves and add to the bread and tomatoes.
Drain some olives and add to the bowl.
Stir to mix all ingredients.
Leave for a few minutes for flavours to develop while you grate the cheese.
Serve the cheese in a separate bowl.

SANDWICHES

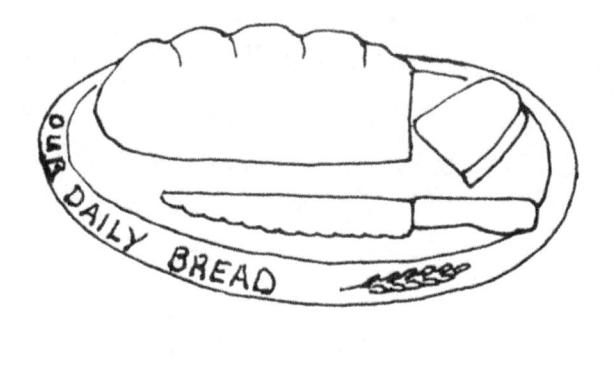

SANDWICHES

Sandwiches may seem an obvious and simple meal that anyone can make but it's easy to fall into habits and produce dull, stodgy food. While bread is filling it's not the most important ingredient and some thought should be made to fillings with taste, nutrition and variety. Open sandwiches reduce the bread and allow the filling to dominate. These are a bit more difficult to eat with the fingers, and as it's a good idea to serve a side-salad, it's best to eat them with a knife and fork.

Here are a few tips to stimulate the imagination:

Always keep your favourite mayonnaise ready in the fridge. It will mix with an endless variety of ingredients and not just egg or tuna.

Tinned fish of any kind is an excellent example. Drained and mashed with a spoonful of mayonnaise; mackerel, smoked mackerel, sardines, or salmon are more flavourful and moist. No need to use any other spread on the bread. If you want to add a little more interest and nutrition a bit of chopped parsley and lemon juice will do the trick.

Leftover meat can be used in the same way. Any dry bits of cooked meat are surprisingly delicious chopped finely, mashed with a fork or whizzed in the food processor with a little mayonnaise and seasoning. For beef, add a little mustard to the mayonnaise for an extra kick.

Crushed garlic is a good addition but not too much or the other flavours will be overpowered.

For turkey or chicken add a little finely chopped stem ginger or ginger syrup for a lovely combination of flavours.

Cheese is an old favourite for a quick sandwich meal. Cheddar is the perfect choice for a sandwich. Organic Cheddar has a better texture and taste.

Try a little grated apple mashed with the cheese or a little chutney or sauce.

For a toasted cheese sandwich Lancashire cheese is ideal. Lancashire cooks perfectly without the oiliness and stringy texture of Cheddar. It's a pale, crumbly cheese which bubbles to a golden brown under the grill. Slightly fiddly to use but worth it. (Little tip: if crumbs of cheese stick to the grill pan rinse it immediately with cold water to loosen it.)

If you enjoy herbs, try adding them finely chopped to the sandwich fillings and experiment with your favourites. Basil is great with cheese and tomato, thyme is good with beef, parsley goes well with most things but especially fish or egg.

Don't be afraid of trying out new things. Just think about what you enjoy the most and experiment with combinations.

Dry Bread Alternatives.

If your loaf has gone dry don't give up on it. Toast is the obvious choice but there are tasty alternatives. For example, if the bread is cubed it can be used to add to salads. Crush a little garlic, if liked, with a little salt and pepper and add to a tablespoon or so of olive oil in a bowl. Add the bread cubes and roll them around to pick up the oil. Then add extra ingredients like grated cheese, tomatoes, chopped boiled egg, olives, chopped herbs, apple pieces etc. in combinations according to taste.

Or, heat a little oil in a frying pan and when the oil is sizzling hot add the bread cubes and brown them gently. Then you can add any leftover vegetables or spinach leaves, chopped mushrooms or tinned sweetcorn. Beat eggs with salt and pepper and pour over the bread and vegetables. Allow the egg to set to make a delicious omelette. Alternatively add tomatoes, cook for a minute or two then turn down the heat and add Lancashire cheese . Allow it to melt briefly and serve.

SOUPS

SOUPS

Soup is very easy to make if you follow basic techniques.

Always use good stock cubes because these form the savoury foundation for the soup and contribute a great deal to the taste. I use organic stock cubes, most often vegetable for soup but occasionally chicken. Don't make the soup too watery or it will be dull and lack a substantial texture.

Invest in a hand blender or the kind of liquidising jug which comes with a food processor. These thicken soups and bulk up the ingredients to make it more satisfying.

Leftovers of any kind make good soups. An odd carrot, parsnip, or celery, for example, can be added to other ingredients to make a flavourful soup. The combinations are endless and it's easy, once you've got the basic method, to make a lovely soup from bits that would otherwise go to waste.

Ingredients like potatoes or lentils can be added for extra taste, texture and nutrition.

Here are a few of my favourites to get you started.

PARSNIP AND CASHEW SOUP

100g Cashew Nuts
1 Onion
2 good sized Carrots
2 good sized Parsnips
1 medium Potato
3 Vegetable Stock Cubes
Bay Leaf (optional)

Grind the cashews finely in a nut mill or food processor.
Chop the onion. Peel and chop carrots, parsnips and the potato.
Put 1200 mls of water into a pan and heat. Stir in the crumbled stock cubes.
Add all the ingredients. Bring to the boil. Reduce heat and simmer for about 20 minutes.
When the vegetables are tender, remove the bay leaf, if used. Allow to cool slightly then blend with a hand blender or liquidiser. Don't overdo the blending if you prefer to have some vegetable pieces in the soup.

This is a thick creamy soup. If it's thicker than you'd like just add a little water or milk.

BEAN AND BASIL SOUP

Slightly fiddly but very tasty. Worth the effort.

100g Bacon
2 Celery sticks
1 or 2 Garlic cloves
2 medium Potatoes
3 Tomatoes
Red Chilli Pepper
Basil leaves
100g dried small Pasta
1 can of Baked Beans
2 Vegetable Stock Cubes

Fry or grill the bacon and cut into small pieces.
Wash and chop the vegetables.
Skin the tomatoes (Easy if you put them in a bowl and fill with boiling water. Leave for a minute, drain, cool in cold water, drain again and remove skin.) Chop them into small pieces.
Chop the chilli finely. (Remember to wash hands immediately afterwards to prevent irritation to eyes).
In a large saucepan gently fry the celery for a minute or two. Add the bacon and vegetables.
Crush the garlic and add to the pan.
Cook for a few minutes.
Add two thirds of the baked beans to the pan.
Add 1200mls water and the crumbled stock cubes. Stir well.
Mash the remaining beans or whiz in a food processor.
Bring the pan to the boil and stir in the pasta. Cook for 12 minutes.
Add the torn basil leaves and the mashed beans and stir well.
Simmer for another 5 minutes, then serve.

CHICKEN SOUP

This is such a satisfying and soothing soup and a brilliant way to use up those raggy bits of leftover chicken. Homemade is out of this world for taste. Variations of this can be made using any odd vegetables as long as you use good chicken stock, either fresh or cubes. I use organic stock cubes if I haven't any stock left over from cooking the chicken. Here's a version to get you going.

Cooked Chicken
1 Onion or Leek
2 Carrots
1 big Parsnip
1 medium Potato
2 Chicken Stock Cubes

Cut the chicken into small pieces, removing meat from bones and discarding skin and gristle.
Chop the onion or leek. Peel carrots, potato and parsnip and dice them.
Put about a litre of water in a saucepan and add the crumbled stock cubes.
Add all the ingredients and bring to the boil. Stir well.
Reduce heat and put a lid on the pan. Simmer for 20 minutes.
Allow to cool then blend just a little to thicken it a bit without losing all of the pieces of chicken and vegetables.

The onion and carrots are basic ingredients. Other things like celery or celeriac can be added for extra taste instead of, or in addition to, parsnips. Red lentils are also a good addition to thicken the soup.

COURGETTE WITH PESTO SOUP

The addition of pesto to this soup makes it extra flavourful but I don't recommend using bought pesto from a jar which has a different and bitter taste. See my recipe for Pesto in CHEESE DISHES section.

2 tablespoons Cashew Nuts
1 Onion
750g Courgette
2 Garlic cloves
2 Vegetable Stock Cubes
8-10 Basil leaves
2 tablespoons homemade Pesto

Grind the nuts in a food processor or nut mill.
Slice the onion and courgettes and add to the processor. Whiz until small pieces have formed.
Heat 750 mls of water and crumble in the stock cubes. Add vegetables, nuts, basil leaves and crushed garlic.
Simmer for 15 minutes.
If you want a thicker soup blend with a hand blender or in a liquidiser jug.
Just before serving, stir the pesto into the soup.

CAKES AND PIES

CAKES AND PIES

CAKES

What could be nicer than a freshly baked cake? The most satisfying are made with simple homely ingredients.

Many cooks still rely on outdated methods. Mrs Beeton, the famous Victorian (who had servants to do her baking) recommended practices which are off-putting and no longer necessary. Even today, surprisingly, her ideas carry weight. They might have been good when cooks used solid lumps of sugar and hard fats but modern ingredients are far better and equipment makes light work of producing a cake.

I have devised simple recipes which give delicious results. I recommend doubling up to save time and make full use of the oven. Surplus can be frozen for another day.

BANANA AND CRANBERRY LOAF

I made this recipe after several disappointments with banana loaves. Every recipe I tried didn't rise, was rubbery and bland. So I came up with my own version and, trust me, it's really good.

The recipe makes two for efficiency but can easily be halved if necessary. Cake liners for the loaf tins make turning out and washing them afterwards very easy.

I use Whitworths cranberries or Ocean Spray "craisins" for this recipe.

4 Bananas
4 large Eggs
150g Caster Sugar
400g Self-raising Flour
2 heaped teaspoons Baking Powder
30g Bran
200g Sunflower Oil
1 packet of dried, sweetened Cranberries

Line two loaf tins with cake liners.

Heat the oven to 180C/160C fan oven

Whiz the bananas in a food processor (or mash until liquid).
Put all other ingredients except the cranberries into a mixing bowl and add the processed bananas.
Mix well to combine then add cranberries and mix a little more to distribute them.
Put the mixture into the loaf tins.
Bake for 40 minutes.
The top will look crusty but will be lovely and moist inside.
Test with a skewer to check the middle is cooked. Leave in the tins until cool enough to turn out. Allow to cool completely. Freeze one.
Serve buttered slices.

FRUIT CAKE

This recipe makes two cakes. You will need a large mixing bowl. An electric hand mixer helps with the mixing. You will need two deep cake tins, approximately 8 inches or 20 cm diameter. Cake liners are a good idea too.

400g Dates
300g Raisins or Sultanas or a mixture of each
540g Self-raising Flour
60g Bran
250g Muscovado Sugar
300g Sunflower Oil
6 large Eggs
Grated rind of an Orange
1 heaped teaspoon Cinnamon
1 heaped teaspoon ground Ginger
1 level teaspoon of ground Cloves

Stone and chop the dates. Put them into a heatproof jug with the raisins. Boil the kettle and pour the water over to almost the top of the fruit. Leave to soak while preparing other ingredients.
Scrub the orange and grate the peel. Add to soaking fruit.
Heat oven to 180C/160C fan oven.
Beat the eggs and sugar together. Add other ingredients including the slightly cooled fruit and liquid.
Mix thoroughly.
Put mixture into the lined cake tins.
Bake for 45 minutes. Test centre with a skewer. If it's sticky, put it back for 2 or 3 more minutes.
It will look very brown on top but that's alright.
Allow to cool enough to turn out of the tins and cool on a wire rack.
Freeze one. Keeps really well.

EASY-PEASY SPONGE CAKE

You will need two greased, loose-bottomed sponge tins.

200g Caster Sugar
200g Self-raising Flour
2 heaped teaspoons Baking Powder
4 large Eggs
200g Sunflower Oil
Butter-cream or Jam for filling

Heat oven to 180C/160C fan oven.
Put all ingredients into a food processor and whiz, or beat with a hand mixer in a baking bowl.
Put mixture evenly into the tins and bake for 20 – 25 minutes.
Press the centre gently. If it springs back it is cooked.
Allow to cool slightly then turn out, using a cake spatula to lift the cakes from the bases.
When completely cool, spread with butter-cream or jam and sandwich cakes together.

GINGER SPONGE CAKE

You will need two greased, loose-bottomed, sponge tins

200 g Caster Sugar
200g Self-raising Flour
2 heaped teaspoons Baking Powder
4 large eggs
200g Sunflower Oil
3 lumps Stem Ginger
1 tablespoon of Ginger Syrup from the jar (see recipe for home-made in PRESERVES)

Chop stem ginger into small pieces.
Heat oven to 180C/160C fan oven.
Put all ingredients except chopped ginger into a food processor and whiz until mixed. Or mix by hand with electric beaters.
Add chopped ginger and briefly pulse or mix to distribute through mixture.
Pour evenly into cake tins and bake for 20 – 25 minutes.
Press the centre gently. If it springs back it's cooked.
Allow to cool a little then turn out of the tins, using a cake spatula to separate cakes from the bases.
The ginger sinks to the bottom of the cakes. That's not a problem.

Good as it is cut into individual slices, or sandwiched with butter icing to make a whole cake.
Also makes a lovely pudding, without icing, served with greek yoghurt.

SWEET-TREAT SQUARES

EASY METHODS FOR INDIVIDUAL CAKES

Buns or cupcakes are a treat to eat but baking them is not easy. Putting the mixture into the tins or paper cases can be a tricky business. It's difficult to spread the mixture evenly between the cases and can result in a sticky mess. Try my method instead to bake square individual cakes with no fuss.

You will need a large roasting tin, measuring approximately 30 x 25 cm (12 x 10 inches). Here are some recipes for my SWEET-TREAT SQUARES.

DATE AND GINGER SQUARES

200g Dates
100 ml Water
Juice of a Lemon or 2 small Lemons
4 large Eggs
200g Caster Sugar
275g Self-raising Flour
10g Bran
2 heaped teaspoons Baking Powder
2 heaped teaspoons ground Ginger
200g Sunflower Oil.

Grease the roasting tin.
Stone and chop dates. Boil the kettle and pour 100ml water into a heatproof jug. Add chopped dates and lemon juice. Leave to soak while mixing other ingredients.
Heat oven to 180C/160C fan oven.
Beat eggs and sugar.
Add flour, bran, baking powder and ginger.
Add oil and dates with soaking liquid.
Beat well.
Put mixture into the tin and bake for 25-30 minutes.
Press centre. If it springs back it's cooked.
Allow to cool in the tin then cut into even squares.
Lift out with a cake spatula.

Also good as individual puddings with greek yoghurt, cream or custard.

ICED AND SPICED SQUARES

These make a good substitute for hot-cross buns at Easter but are good at any time. My favourites.

Grease a roasting tin.

140g Raisins or Sultanas or a mixture of the two
50g Candied Peel, chopped fine
100ml boiling Water
200g Caster Sugar
4 large Eggs
200g Self-raising Flour
20g Bran
1 teaspoon ground Ginger
1 teaspoon ground Cloves
1 teaspoon Cinnamon
2 teaspoons Baking Powder
1 tablespoon dried Milk
200g Sunflower Oil
Icing Sugar

Boil the kettle and pour 100ml of water into a heatproof jug. Add raisins and peel and leave to soak.
Heat oven to 180C/160 fan oven.
Mix other ingredients then add soaked fruit and soaking liquid. Mix well.
Spread in greased tin and bake for 25-30 minutes.
Press centre. If it springs back it's cooked.
Allow to cool completely .
Mix icing sugar with a few drops of water to a thick but spreadable consistency. Spread over the top of the baked cake.
Cut into squares. Allow the icing to set then lift out with a cake spatula.

APPLE AND CINNAMON SQUARES

The cinnamon in these is optional. If you love cinnamon it's a brilliant combination of flavours. If not, the squares are delicious with just the apple. Good for using windfalls if you have apples in the garden or a generous friend.

Cooking Apples
200g Caster Sugar
4 large Eggs
200g Self-raising Flour
2 rounded teaspoons Baking Powder
30g Bran
200g Sunflower Oil
3 tablespoons Sugar for sprinkling
2 – 3 teaspoons ground Cinnamon (optional)

A roasting tin with a vitreous enamel surface is best for this to prevent the apples reacting with metal. Most roasting tins have this.
Grease the roasting tin.
Have a bowl of salted water ready (approx 1 tablespoon salt to 500ml of water) and prepare the apples.
Slice peeled and cored apples into the salted water. Make sure all slices are coated by the salty water to prevent browning.
Beat eggs and sugar together. Add flour, baking powder, bran and oil. Mix well.
Heat oven to 180C/160C fan oven.
Rinse apples and drain, then place slices in the roasting tin.
Sprinkle the 3 tablespoons of sugar, and cinnamon if using, over the apples.
Spread the cake mixture evenly over the apples.
The mixture might feel a little stiff but the juice from the apples will moisten it while it cooks.
Bake for 30 minutes.
Press the centre of the cake. If it springs back it's cooked.
Allow to cool completely before cutting into squares.
Lift out with a palette knife (cake spatula).
Freeze well.

These are even better when a day or two old and make a lovely pudding with cream or greek yoghurt.

SUPER-QUICK BROWNIES

Use a good cocoa powder for these, not drinking chocolate. I use Green and Blacks for its rich chocolate taste. I use oat milk for my baking but most people will use dairy. Either is fine.

Grease a roasting tin

4 large Eggs
200g Caster Sugar
200g Self-raising Flour
2 heaped teaspoons Baking Powder
4 heaped tablespoons Cocoa Powder
4 tablespoons Milk
200g Sunflower Oil

Heat oven to 180C/160C fan oven
Put all ingredients into a food processor and whiz to mix. Alternatively, put them all in a bowl and mix with an electric hand mixer.
Put mixture into the tin.
Bake for 20 – 25 minutes.
Press centre. If it springs back it's cooked.
Allow to cool then cut into squares. Lift out with a palette knife.

Good as they are but if you like a sweeter treat, try one of these:

Spread with jam or marmalade. Cherry jam is especially good for a Black Forest taste.
Slice and fill with Buttercream (vanilla, chocolate, with or without nuts)
Glace icing on top, with or without nuts or glace cherries.
Melted chocolate.

FREDA MAXFIELD

CHOC AND GINGER SQUARES

Grease a large roasting tin.

5 large Eggs
200g Brown Sugar
200g Self-raising Flour
2 heaped teaspoons Baking Powder
2 teaspoons ground Ginger
3 tablespoons Cocoa
200g Sunflower Oil
1 tablespoon Milk

Heat oven to 180C/160C fan oven

Beat eggs and sugar together. Add other ingredients and mix well.
Put mixture into the roasting tin.
Bake for 20 – 25 minutes.
Press centre. If it springs back it's cooked.
Leave to cool then cut into squares. Lift out with a palette knife.

GINGER SQUARES

4 large Eggs
125g Brown Sugar
3 tablespoons Golden Syrup
200g Self-raising Flour
30g Bran
2 heaped teaspoons Baking Powder
2 teaspoons ground Ginger
200g Sunflower Oil
Marmalade (optional)

Grease a roasting tin
Heat oven to 180C/160C fan oven

Beat eggs and sugar together. Add golden syrup and beat again.
Add dry ingredients and oil. Mix well.
Put the mixture into the tin.
Bake for 20 minutes.
Press centre of cake. If it springs back it's cooked. Or insert a skewer. If it comes out dry it's cooked.
Allow to cool in the tin.
Cut into squares and lift out with a palette knife.
If using marmalade, spread on top of the cakes.

LEMON SQUARES

2 Lemons
200g Caster Sugar
4 large Eggs
200g Self-raising Flour
20g Bran
2 heaped teaspoons Baking Powder
200g Sunflower Oil

Grease a roasting tin. Heat oven to 180C/160C fan oven.
Scrub the lemons. Grate one and juice both. You will need 50ml of juice.
Put all ingredients into a mixing bowl and beat well until combined.
Put mixture into the roasting tin.
Bake for 20 – 22 minutes.
Test the centre with a skewer. It will come out clean if cooked.
Allow to cool then cut into squares. Lift out with a palette knife.

Good as they are but lovely with icing, marmalade or lemon curd on top.

CRANBERRY AND ORANGE SQUARES

100g Dried, sweetened Cranberries
1 Orange
4 large Eggs
200g Caster Sugar
200g Self-raising Flour
2 heaped teaspoons Baking Powder
20g Bran
200g Sunflower Oil

Grease a roasting tin.
Put the cranberries in a heatproof jug and just cover with boiling water. Not higher than the fruit. Leave to soak.
Grate the orange peel.
Heat the oven to 180C/160C fan oven.
Put the other ingredients in a mixing bowl and beat.
Add the grated orange zest and the cranberries with the water. Mix well.
Spread the mixture in the roasting tin.
Bake for 30 minutes.
Test with a skewer. If it's sticky, replace in the oven for a minute or two.

This can be done with lemon instead. Just add the dried cranberries to the recipe above for LEMON SQUARES.

PARSNIP SQUARES

Parsnip, approximately 200g before preparation
4 large Eggs
200g Caster Sugar
200g Self-raising Flour
2 heaped teaspoons Baking Powder
30g Bran
200g Sunflower Oil

Peel the parsnip and grate it or chop finely in a food processor.
Heat the oven to 180C/160C fan oven. Grease a large baking tin or roaster, 30 x 25cm(12 x 10 inches)
Put all the ingredients, including the parsnip bits, into a bowl and mix well.
Spread in the tin and bake for 25 minutes. Test with a skewer to see if the middle is cooked.
If not, allow a few more minutes in the oven.
Allow to cool and cut into squares.
Freeze well.

PASTRY

I have an easy formula for making pastry. It's not ideal for rolling out but it presses well into the baking dish and is ideal when you only need a pastry base. It will also cut into small shapes, for eg. mince pies or jam tarts. Try it. You might like it as much as I do.

You will need a set of cup measures.

To make one pastry base for a flan dish approximately 22.5cm (8 inches)

Grease the flan dish

1 cup Plain Flour
1 third of a cup Sunflower Oil
1 quarter of a cup of cold Water

Put all the ingredients into a food processor and whiz until combined.
Switch off and remove the lump of pastry. Squeeze a little if necessary.
With clean fingers, press into the greased dish, making sure all the surface is covered and up the sides.
Pop into the fridge while you make the filling to prevent the oil from separating.

If you're baking "blind", ie. pre-baking before adding filling, prick the surface of the pastry all over with a sharp fork and chill for about 20 minutes in the fridge before baking for 9 minutes at 190C/170C fan oven. Then add filling and bake again for the required time.

The pastry base can be filled with sweet or savoury ingredients. See recipes below.

FREDA MAXFIELD

NECTARINE FLAN

Pastry base. See instructions above.

5 juicy Nectarines
100g Breadcrumbs
3 tablespoons Sugar

Sprinkle crumbs over the pastry base.
Wash, stone and slice nectarines.
Heat oven to 190C/170C fan oven
Arrange sliced nectarines in a circle pattern in the dish, covering as much of the breadcrumbs as possible.
Sprinkle the sugar carefully over the fruit. If the fruit seems a bit dry, sprinkle a little water over to dissolve the sugar.
Bake for 30 minutes.

Allow to cool and serve with vanilla ice-cream.

PECAN PIE

This is a sensationally rich dessert, very sweet and full of delicious flavour. Not difficult to make, freezes well and always impresses guests.

Note. If the bag of pecans look broken it's a good idea to have extra in order to have enough perfect ones for decorating.

1 cup Plain Flour
Third of a cup Sunflower Oil
Quarter of a cup of cold Water
3 large Eggs
Three quarters of a cup of Caster Sugar
1 cup Golden Syrup
250g Pecan Nut halves
1 cup of broken Pecans from the 250g bag
20g soft Butter
Half teaspoon Salt

Grease a 22.5 cm (about 8 inch) flan dish.
Make the pastry by putting the flour, sunflower oil and cold water into a food processor. Whiz to combine. Switch off and remove all the pastry. Squeeze a little if necessary. Press into the flan dish making sure all the base and up the sides are covered. Place the dish in the fridge while you make the filling.
Tip the pecans out onto a clean surface or plate. Select good halves and reserve them for decorating. Remove broken ones, break into small pieces and put into a cup measure.
Heat oven to 190C/170C fan oven.
When the measure is generously full, tip the nuts into the food processor (no need to wash the processor after making the pastry). Grind finely and leave in the processor.
Add eggs, sugar, golden syrup, salt and butter to the ground pecans and whiz well to combine.
Pour mixture into the pastry case.
Now for the tricky bit! Arrange whole pecan halves around the top in a circular pattern by dropping them gently onto the mixture. They will float on top with a little care and look fabulous.
Carry the flan dish very carefully to the oven and bake for about 35

minutes. Best to use a timer to prevent the nuts from burning.

It will become dark brown and may bubble a bit during baking but should flatten again when it's cooling.

Allow to go cold so that it will set.

Serve cold or slightly reheated with cream or vanilla ice-cream.

Freezes really well so a good one to make ahead for a special occasion.

See photos for stages of making this in "Christmas Thoughts" on my blog, www.earthyhomemakernet.wordpress.com

PUDDINGS

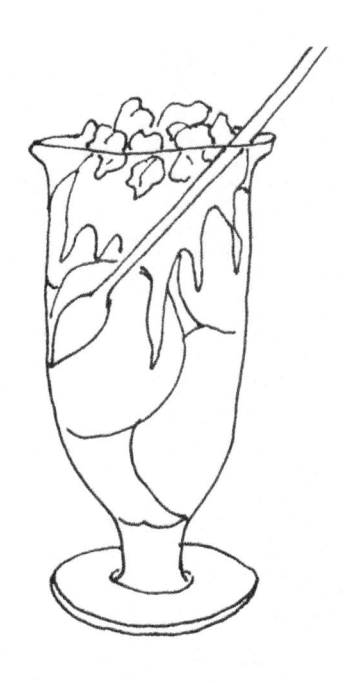

PUDDINGS

APPLE POBS PUDDING

When I was child, if I was feeling unwell, my mother would make something we called "pobs". This was bread soaked in warm, sweetened milk. Soothing and easy to eat. This pudding is based on this with the addition of egg and apples. Satisfying, simple and delicious.

I use a white bloomer loaf for this. It has the right texture and the crusts crisp beautifully on the top.

2 Cooking Apples
300mls Milk
4 tablespoons Sugar
1 large Egg
Half a loaf of Bread
A small amount of butter

Peel and slice the apples into salted water, making sure the surfaces are coated to prevent browning.
Heat the oven to 190C/170C fan oven.
Warm the milk a little. Beat in the egg and two tablespoons of the sugar.
Break the bread into pieces and put half in a baking dish.
Pour half the milk mixture over the bread.
Rinse and drain the apples and arrange over the bread in the dish.
Sprinkle the rest of the sugar over the apples.
Put the rest of the bread pieces on top of the apples.
Carefully pour the remaining milk mixture over and press down gently to soak the bread.
Dot with butter.
Bake for 25 - 30 minutes.

Delicious hot or cold.

BANANA CUSTARD PUDDING

This is a good way of using up ripe bananas and bread which has gone dry.

2 ripe small Bananas
Half a loaf of Bread
300ml Milk
2 large Eggs
2 - 3 tablespoons Sugar

Heat the oven to 190C/170C fan oven.
Whiz the bananas in a food processor until smooth.
Break the bread into pieces.
Put the broken bread pieces in a baking dish.
Warm the milk a little. Add to the bananas with the sugar and eggs.
Whiz to combine.
Pour the milk and banana mixture over the bread.
Allow to soak for a few minutes.
Bake for 25 - 30 minutes until golden brown on top.

Good hot or cold.

CHRISTMAS PUDDINGS

If you like Christmas pudding but have been put off making them by the thought of steaming them for hours, then consider these. They steam in the oven under foil for two hours. No steamy kitchen!

These are short-term individual puddings. They will keep for about three months in greaseproof paper in a tin but they are best frozen. They will keep for at least a year in the freezer and thaw quickly. The fruitier ingredients and spices can be adjusted to suit your taste.

You will need individual pudding tins, a large, deep roasting tin and aluminium foil.
Makes about 8 - 10

200g Self-raising Flour
2 teaspoons Spice (I use cinnamon, cloves and ground ginger)
Pinch of Salt
150g Breadcrumbs
50g Pecans, chopped
2 cooking or sharp Apples
300g Raisins
300g Sultanas
80g (approximately) of a mixture of chopped stem ginger, grated orange and lemon peel and candied peel
4 large Eggs
Juice of 2 lemons
2 tablespoons of Black Treacle
350g Dark Sugar
150g Butter
4 tablespoons of Rum or Brandy (or a mixture of both)

Finely chop the stem ginger and candied peel.
Zest the orange and 1 lemon and mix with the ginger and candied peel to make approximately 80g. The proportions can be adjusted according to your taste preference.

Put these into a large mixing bowl.
Grind the pecans or chop finely and add to the bowl.
Add raisins and sultanas.
Mix flour, spices, salt and breadcrumbs.
Add to the other ingredients.
Beat the eggs. Add black treacle and the juice of the lemons.
Melt the butter and stir in sugar. Add to the mixing bowl with the egg mixture.
Add the rum and/or brandy.
Mix thoroughly for several minutes.
Leave to stand for 30 minutes or longer.
Heat the oven to 190C/170C fan oven.
Stir mixture again and spoon into greased pudding basins.
Stand the basins in a large, deep roasting tin and cover each one with foil.
Boil a full kettle and pour the hot water around the tins to about a third of their height.
Cover the top of the roaster with another large piece of foil and tuck in around the edges.
Carry very carefully to the oven to prevent water from splashing out. Bake for 2 hours.
When the time is up remove carefully from the oven and allow to cool before removing foil.
Lift the puddings out of the water.
When the puddings are cool, slide a knife around them to loosen and tip out.
I serve these with Rum Sauce. See my SAUCES section for the recipe.

Each pudding takes one minute in the microwave from frozen.

QUICK FIX PUDDINGS

My cake squares make good puddings, hot or cold. The crumby texture goes well with custard, yoghurt, cream or ice-cream. The Apple and Cinnamon are especially good.

My Ginger Sponge makes an excellent cold pudding with Greek-style yoghurt.

Plain sponge cake is great with a dollop of home-made jam. Serve with custard, cream or Greek-style yoghurt.

See my CAKES section for these.

SWEET TREAT DESSERTS

ICE-CREAM WITH TOASTED PECANS AND HOT CHOCOLATE SAUCE

This is always a favourite and so easy to make. Use good quality cocoa powder but not drinking chocolate. I don't add sugar. I prefer the contrast between the dark chocolate and the sweet ice-cream and also sugar might make the sauce burn in the micro-wave.

Vanilla Ice-cream
Pecan Nuts
Cocoa Powder
Milk

Break the nuts into pieces and spread in a roasting tin. Heat the grill.
Toast the nuts under the hot grill for a few minutes. Don't let them burn but they will become dark brown. Allow to cool.

To make the sauce, put a couple of tablespoons of cocoa powder into a jug and pour on a little milk. Stir to mix until a smooth, thick, but runny consistency is reached. Add a little more milk if necessary.
Microwave for a minute. The sauce will thicken.

Stir well.

Put the ice-cream into dishes (tall ones look best), pour the hot chocolate sauce over and sprinkle the toasted pecans on top.

FREDA MAXFIELD

ICE-CREAM WITH GINGER SYRUP

Vanilla Ice-cream or Greek-style Yoghurt
Ginger Syrup

Drizzle the ginger syrup over the ice-cream or yoghurt for a sensational combination.
Ginger syrup is available from a jar of stem ginger or see my recipe in PRESERVING.

WALNUT AND COFFEE CREAM ROULADE

For this you will need a hand mixer (electric beaters), a swiss roll tin (12 x 8 "/ 30 x 20cm approx.) and a roll of greaseproof paper.

50g Plain Flour
2 large Eggs
65g Caster Sugar
50g Walnuts plus a few for decoration
Strong Coffee
300mls Whipping Cream
Icing Sugar

Line the greased tin with greaseproof paper. Bring it slightly up above the edges and crease the corners.
Break the 50g of walnuts into small pieces.
Heat the oven to 220C/200C fan oven.
Beat eggs and sugar together. Add nuts and beat really well until the mixture has significantly increased in volume. The beater should ideally leave a trail in the mixture. Takes a few minutes.
Sift the flour into the mixture and fold in gently with a metal spoon.
Spread in the lined tin and bake for 7-8 minutes.
While it bakes, spread a sheet of greaseproof paper on the worktop and sprinkle lightly with caster sugar.
When the cake is ready, tip the tin upside down onto the paper. Leave for a minute then gently peel away the lining paper. Roll up the cake using the shorter edge of the greaseproof sheet, enclosing the paper.
Allow to cool completely.
Make a small amount of very strong coffee. Sieve it if using ground coffee. Leave to cool completely.
Add one and a half tablespoons of icing sugar to the cream. Beat until almost stiff, taking care not to over beat. Stir in a tablespoon of the coffee.
Gently unroll the cake. It may split but don't worry.
Spread half the cream over the cake and roll up with the cream

inside.

Place on a serving plate and decorate the top with cream and walnut halves.

Will freeze well. To freeze, leave the filled and decorated cake on the greaseproof paper. Slide a baking sheet underneath the paper and open freeze. When it's solid wrap the cake in the paper and place in a suitable container or foil wrap then replace in the freezer.

Unwrap while frozen and thaw on a suitable serving plate in the fridge.

GINGER CREAM ROULADE

You will need a hand mixer (electric beaters), a swiss roll tin (12 x 8"/30 x 20cm approx.) and a roll of greaseproof paper.

3 large Eggs
75g Caster Sugar
75g Plain Flour
2 lumps Stem Ginger
2 teaspoons of Syrup from the Stem Ginger
300 mls Whipping Cream
Half a tablespoon Caster Sugar

Line the greased tin with greaseproof paper bringing the edges up above the sides slightly.
Chop the stem ginger into small pieces.
Heat the oven to 200C/180C fan oven.
Beat the eggs and sugar until a slight trail is left in the mixture. Takes a few minutes.
Sift the flour into the eggs and sugar and gently fold in with a metal spoon.
Spread the mixture in the lined tin and bake for 10 to 12 minutes until golden and springs back.
While the cake cooks spread a sheet of greaseproof paper on the worktop and sprinkle lightly with caster sugar.
When the cake is ready, leave for a minute to cool slightly.
Roll up the cake enclosing the sheet of greaseproof paper and leave to cool completely.
Beat the whipping cream with the half tablespoon of sugar until nearly stiff. Take care not to over beat. Stir in the ginger pieces and two teaspoons of ginger syrup.
Gently unroll the cake. It may split but don't worry.
Spread half the cream over the cake and reroll enclosing the cream.
Place on a serving plate and decorate the top with remaining cream.

Will freeze well. To freeze, leave the filled and decorated cake on the greaseproof paper and slide a baking sheet underneath the paper. Open freeze, then when it's solid wrap in the paper and place in a suitable container or foil wrap.

Unwrap while still frozen and thaw on a serving plate in the fridge.

FRUIT TREATS

STRAWBERRIES

During the Summer I enjoy plenty of homegrown Strawberries and I freeze any surplus.
However, thawed strawberries lose flavour and texture and are disappointing to eat. My remedy is to cook them in their own juice and add sugar to taste. This transforms a disappointment into a delicious dessert to enjoy with Greek-style yoghurt or vanilla ice-cream.

Allow to thaw in the cooking pan and heat gently once the juice has run. Best not to add water but if they begin to stick add a drop or two to moisten. When they're hot stir in the sugar a little at a time until the desired sweetness is obtained. Allow to cook for about 15 to 20 minutes, until the colour deepens. Allow to cool then serve with yoghurt or ice-cream.

Looks special in a tall glass dish.

NECTARINES

Often supermarket nectarines are under-ripe, hard and sour. They sometimes deteriorate before they've had time to ripen. Cooked, they're a different story. Even hard ones, stoned and sliced into a pan with a little water and stewed gently for about 15 minutes until tender, then sweetened, are a real treat.
Allow the fruit to tenderise then stir in sugar to taste and cook for a few more minutes.

Good hot with ice-cream but also really tasty when cold.

Lovely with ice-cream, sponge cake or yoghurt.

PLUMS

Exactly the same as with nectarines above. The cooking brings out a truly delicious flavour in under-ripe disappointing fruit.

SAUCES

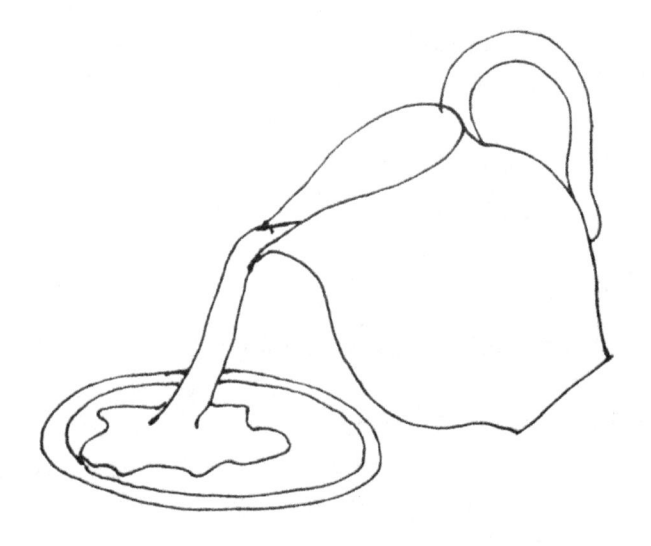

SAUCES

BASIC WHITE SAUCE

This is a useful sauce for puddings or savoury dishes and is very simple to make.

Milk
Cornflour

Sugar or Salt and Pepper

Use sufficient milk by estimating the amount of sauce you will need, but roughly a pint/660 mls to a heaped tablespoon of cornflour.
Heat the milk. While it's warming, mix the cornflour in a jug with another drop of milk to make a smooth, thick, but runny consistency.
Bring the milk to the boil and stir the cornflour into it briskly. Turn the heat down a little but keep stirring until the sauce thickens.

For SWEET sauce, stir in a tablespoon of sugar.

For SAVOURY sauce, add salt and pepper.

If the sauce is thicker than you'd like, stir in a little extra milk.

Useful as it is but you can add ingredients. For eg. to make RUM SAUCE add a tablespoon of rum to the basic sweet sauce. This is delicious with Christmas pudding as a good alternative to brandy butter.

CHEESE SAUCE
For a cheese sauce add grated Cheddar or crumbled Lancashire cheese to the basic savoury sauce and stir until a creamy consistency is reached. Good with pasta, on toast, baked potatoes or over vegetables.

ONION SAUCE

For onion sauce, chop an onion finely and cook gently in a small amount of olive oil in a saucepan. Don't allow the onion to brown. Add the milk when the onion is sufficiently soft and bring to the boil.
Make the cornflour paste as given above and add while stirring until the sauce thickens.
Reduce heat and cook gently for a minute.
Add salt and pepper.
Good with sausages or bacon.

MUSTARD SAUCE

Make the basic white sauce as above, add salt and pepper and stir in a little mustard. Good with beef or ham. (To make the mustard, add a few drops of water to two teaspoons of mustard powder and mix to a paste.)

CHOCOLATE SAUCE

This is a quick and easy method of making chocolate sauce. It's delicious with vanilla ice-cream.

Cocoa Powder
Milk
Sugar (optional)

Mix a couple of tablespoons of cocoa powder with a little milk in a microwaveable jug. Make a thick but runny consistency. Add a little milk as the cocoa powder is absorbed.
Microwave for about a minute. It will thicken.
If you prefer it sweet add the sugar after cooking, stirring it in well to mix.
Pour over vanilla ice-cream.
Best hot. It thickens and sets when cold but can be brought back with a few seconds in the microwave.

See SWEET TREAT DESSERTS in my PUDDINGS section for a delicious way to use this.

MINT SAUCE

If you've only had mint sauce in a jar from a shop you have never tasted mint sauce! The difference in the taste of freshly made is sensational and delicious. Very easy to make. If you have mint in the garden, make enough to freeze. When it thaws it tastes just like fresh.

A bunch of Mint (Apple Mint or Spearmint are best)
Malt Vinegar
Sugar

Wash the mint and strip the leaves from the stems. Discard the stems.
Whiz the leaves in a food processor. Alternatively, chop finely and put in a bowl.
Add vinegar to cover the leaves and mix well. Add sugar a little at a time until it reaches the desired sweetness. Now allow it to stand for a few minutes to blend the flavours.

If you make enough to freeze, put into small containers, leaving a gap at the top for expansion. Put on the lids and store in the freezer. Brilliant during Winter when mint isn't available in the garden. Thaws very quickly.

PEANUT SAUCE

This is a microwave recipe but would work in a saucepan on the hob. It's truly delicious and goes perfectly with chicken, sausages or my sausage meatballs.

1 small Onion
1 Garlic Clove
4 teaspoons Lemon Juice from a small Lemon
300mls Water
6 tablespoons of smooth Peanut Butter
1 tablespoon Light Brown Sugar
Half or 1 teaspoon Chilli Powder (depending on how hot you like it)
1 level tablespoon Tomato Puree
Salt and Pepper

Chop the onion finely, crush the garlic clove, juice the lemon and put them in a microwaveable bowl. Add the other ingredients and stir well.
Microwave on high for 6 minutes or until the sauce is boiling and thickening.
Remove and stir.
Reduce the setting to Low and cook again for about 5 minutes more.

Good served hot or cold. It thickens a lot more when cold but is still really tasty and enjoyable.

APPLE SAUCE

It's best to use cooking apples because they melt in the pan when heated. This is a versatile sauce. It's good with pork or chicken but it's also delicious as a dessert with custard, yoghurt or ice-cream. Can be used for an excellent pie filling. Simple to make and can be frozen.

Cooking Apples
Sugar
Salt

Wash, peel and core the apples and slice into salted water. (About 1 tablespoon salt to 500 mls water). Make sure the apples are coated by the salt water to prevent the surfaces from browning.
When all the apples are ready, rinse and drain in a colander. They will not taste salty.
Tip into a saucepan and add a small amount of water.
Turn up the heat and stir occasionally to prevent sticking or burning.
As the apples "fall" reduce the heat and continue to stir.
When the apples are mushy add sugar a little at a time and taste until it's as sweet as you like.

Can be eaten hot or cold as a dessert or allowed to cool to use with a meat meal. Especially good with sage and onion stuffing.

CRANBERRY SAUCE

If you have only tried this sauce from a bought jar you haven't experienced the full pleasure of cranberry sauce. The real thing is so simple to make and freezes perfectly. I make it ahead at Christmas and thaw it as I need to. It is wonderful with turkey but delicious with many other meats, bacon or vegetarian meals. See my FESTIVE FLAN recipe in VEGETARIAN MEALS

Cranberries, fresh or frozen
Sugar

If using fresh cranberries, pick them over and remove any mushy ones as these will taste mouldy.
Wash well and place in a saucepan with a small amount of water. Bring to the boil then reduce heat and cook for about half an hour until the fruit is softened. Best to put on a lid as the cranberries often burst as they cook.
When the fruit is tender, add a little water if necessary and stir in sugar. Add the sugar a little at a time and taste until it's sweet enough. Cranberries need a lot of sugar.
Cook gently until the sugar and fruit juice has combined.
Allow to cool. It will set with a jam-like texture when cold.

Will freeze in plastic containers and is just like fresh when thawed.

PRESERVING

PRESERVING

A cupboard full of home preserves is a joy to behold, resourceful and satisfying. If you have your own garden produce or fresh from a friend's garden, even better.

Jam making is relatively simple once you've learnt the technique. Surplus fruit can be frozen and saved for making jam in the winter and can result in an endless combination of delicious flavours.

There are recipes galore in other cookbooks for chutneys and pickles. Here I give you a small selection of mine and methods for preserving other foods. They work, are easy to do and keep well.

PRACTICAL ADVICE

Preserving is not difficult but requires organisation and time set aside for the job. The following advice will become clear with each recipe but is worth noting before you begin.

In order to preserve food it's best to have a few items of equipment on hand for the purpose. These should always be kept perfectly clean to prevent spoilage from bacteria or moulds.

Old jam, mayonnaise, or coffee jars are fine for chutneys providing they are scrupulously cleaned of their old contents, labels carefully removed and lids in perfect condition. Never use a rusty lid because the vinegar will react to the metal. Plastic coated lids are best for vinegary pickles.

Special preserving jars of the Kilner or mason type with sealing lids and rings should be used for bottling fruit or tomatoes. This is a bit more specialised so requires more skill and detailed instructions.

Never attempt to bottle vegetables such as beans without a special pressure cooker and precise instructions. Very poisonous Botulism can result if these are not processed and sealed at very high temperatures. If you think you could do this, research the methods and equipment thoroughly first.

Wooden spoons with very long handles are available for making jam or chutney. They keep your wrist and arm out of reach of the hot bubbling contents of the pan. Boiling jam on skin is very painful. One spoon for jam and another for chutney is recommended to prevent oniony, vinegary, flavours from mingling.

A soup ladle is useful for transferring chutney or jam into jars.

A funnel is also another bit of kit which enables you to keep the outside of the jars clean during the ladling. The mouth should be wide enough to take lumpy substances but just narrow enough to fit inside the tops of jars.

When making chutney or jam, jars need to be washed first in hot sudsy water then thoroughly rinsed before placing in the oven and warmed on a low temperature while the jam or chutney is cooking.

Lids need to be washed, rinsed and dried on kitchen paper before putting somewhere warm to continue drying. Best not to put these in the oven as most lids have a plastic coating inside.

When hot jars are removed from the oven to be filled it's important to prevent them touching a cold surface. This would cause thermal shock and could crack the jars. A large chopping board covered with a little newspaper and/or kitchen paper is ideal for this. If a board is not available a folded teatowel will serve the same purpose. Place it next to the hob if possible, so you can keep the preserve hot while you fill jars.

Lids should be tightly screwed on immediately, while the contents are hot. Don't fill the jar right to the top. Leave a small gap. A vacuum will form as the jar cools which will seal the lid on if this has been done carefully. A popping sound when the jar is cooling indicates that sealing has taken place.

COURGETTE CHUTNEY

Makes about 4 jars

500g Courgettes
2 Cucumbers
150g prepared Runner or French Beans
300g Onions
200g prepared Apples
2 cloves Garlic
700mls Malt Vinegar
1 dessertspoon Mustard Powder
1 teaspoon Chilli Powder
1 heaped teaspoon Celery Salt
4 teaspoons Mustard Seeds
1 heaped teaspoon ground Ginger
300g Golden Sugar
Sea Salt

Wash and cut up the vegetables and apples into small chunks. Place in a large ceramic or stainless steel bowl and sprinkle with sea salt. Cover and leave for 2-3 hours.

While the vegetables are salting, wash and thoroughly rinse the jars and lids. Place the jars in the oven and turn heat to low. Dry lids with kitchen paper and leave somewhere warm to dry. Don't place lids in the oven as most will have a plastic inner coating.

Drain the salty liquid from the vegetables and place in a large cooking pan.

Mix the mustard powder to a runny paste with a little of the vinegar.

Put the rest of the vinegar in the pan. Add the dry ingredients and the mustard paste. Stir well to mix.

Bring to the boil, turn down heat to medium and cook for about 1 and a half hours until it thickens.

Ladle into hot jars, leaving a small gap at the top and tighten lids immediately.

DARK AND SWEET CHUTNEY

Makes about 6 jars.

1kg Courgettes
600g Tomatoes
200g prepared Apples
700g Onions
2 cloves Garlic, crushed
1 red Chilli, finely chopped
600mls Malt Vinegar
1 teaspoon Salt
1 teaspoon Mustard Powder
1 tablespoon Paprika
1 teaspoon Celery Salt
2 teaspoons Mustard Seeds
450g Brown Sugar
110g Raisins

Wash and prepare the apples, garlic and chilli. Chop the courgettes, tomatoes, apples and onions.
Put all ingredients into a large pan and stir well to combine.
Bring slowly to the boil then turn heat to moderate and cook gently for about 2 hours until thickened. Stir now and then to prevent sticking.
While it cooks, wash jars and lids, rinse thoroughly and place jars in the oven. Turn heat to low.

Don't put lids in the oven because some will have a plastic coated interior. Dry these with kitchen paper and put them somewhere warm.

Prepare a surface as near to the hob as possible. Put newspaper covered with kitchen paper onto the surface used or place a folded teatowel over it instead. This will prevent the hot jars contacting a cold surface which could crack them.
Wash and dry a ladle and funnel and keep clean until needed.
When the chutney has thickened, remove jars one by one from the

oven and insert the funnel.

Ladle the hot chutney into the jars, leaving a couple of centimetres empty at the top of each.

Tighten the lids immediately and as the jars cool they will seal. A popping sound indicates that they have sealed successfully. It doesn't matter if they don't seal because the chutney should keep for several months in a cool dark cupboard. Use unsealed jars first as the sealed ones will keep longer.

PICALILLI

You need about 2kg of vegetables when mixed together.
If French beans are not available use runner beans cut into small pieces or frozen green beans.

Cauliflower
Cucumber
Courgette
Onions
French Beans

2 – 4 Chillies, depending on how hot you want it.
1 teaspoon Ground Ginger
30g of plain Flour
2 pints of Malt Vinegar
30g Turmeric
30g Mustard powder
60g Sugar
Sea Salt

Prepare vegetables: Chop onions. Break cauliflower into small florets and discard the stalk. Cut courgette and cucumber into small cubes, no need to peel. Cut beans into small pieces.
Sprinkle them with sea salt. Cover with a cloth or a large plate and leave for 24 hours.

Next day, drain well.

Sterilise jars and lids by washing and rinsing well. Put jars into the oven on a low temperature to dry. Dry lids well with kitchen paper and put somewhere clean and warm to dry (not in the oven).

Chop chillies. Wash hands well after chopping to prevent injury to eyes.
Mix mustard and flour to a runny paste with a little of the vinegar. Put the rest of the vinegar to boil with turmeric, chillies, sugar and ground ginger.
Pour in the mustard paste, stirring well.

Add vegetables and boil for 5- 10 minutes, depending on how soft or crunchy you like it.

Have a surface ready next to the stove with a padding of newspaper or folded teatowels to stand the hot jars on. This will stop the jars from touching a cold surface and prevent them from cracking.

While still hot, fill jars using a funnel to keep rims clean. Screw lids on tightly to seal.

Lids will make a popping sound and be slightly sucked in if they have sealed. If not the picalilli will still keep well but best used as soon as possible. If sealed it will keep well for months in a cool dark place.

MIXED FRUIT JAM

Over the Summer it's a good idea to freeze any surplus fruit from the garden or while it's cheap in the shops. If you have generous friends with fruit to spare but you have no time to use it, just wash and freeze it for making jam on a miserable Winter day.

When I pick fruit from the garden I use whatever I need for a meal and pop any extra bits into the freezer. Then when the weather is horrible I gather all my bits of different fruit, weigh them and thaw them to make jam. It's easy to do with an equal amount of sugar to the total weight of fruit.

Each batch of mixed fruit jam will be different depending on what you've saved and it will be truly delicious. Most fruit flavours mix well.

Windfall apples are excellent for combining with other fruits, especially those with little pectin like strawberries. The apples are rich in pectin which is essential for setting.

Summer fruits such as strawberries, raspberries , gooseberries and nectarines are really good mixed together and I have often added blueberries and cherries to make a tasty and textured preserve.

Plums which are sour, mixed with cooking apples, make a delicious jam because the added sugar sweetens them while keeping a piquancy which is really pleasing. This is an excellent starter jam because it's easy to set.

Misshapen and bruised fruit can be used but it's essential to cut away any damaged areas. Always wash them well before stewing gently in a little water to tenderise and break down the fruit before adding sugar. Sugar needs to be stirred in and dissolved before the contents of the pan are brought to the boil. Then boil rapidly, stirring occasionally to prevent sticking until a setting point is reached. Test for a set by placing a spoonful on a cold plate. Allow it to cool for a few minutes then push it gently. If it wrinkles it's ready. If not, continue boiling until it does.

See general instructions on PRESERVING at the beginning of the chapter for equipment, helpful tips and how to seal jars.

PRESERVED GINGER (STEM GINGER)

This is very easy to do at home and it's not expensive. The preserved ginger can be added to baking, desserts, whipped cream, starters or savoury meals. The syrup is equally versatile. It can be made sweeter and heavier if the bigger quantity of sugar is used (see ingredients). Pour it over ice-cream, add to cake recipes or to savoury dishes.

I use a pressure cooker for this but it can be done in a saucepan, just more slowly.

500g approximately of Root Ginger
800g - 1kg Sugar

Wash and thoroughly rinse a couple of jam jars with sound lids or preserving jars with lids and rings. Also do the same with a couple of small bottles for any excess syrup.
Place the jars and bottles in the oven and turn heat to low.
Dry lids with kitchen paper and leave somewhere warm but not in the oven. If not pressure cooking, leave this stage until the sugar is added.
Wash and peel the ginger root. Making sure all peel is removed. Cut into chunks.
Pressure cook in 1,100mls water, without sugar, for 10 minutes at medium pressure. Allow the cooker to cool gradually to release pressure before removing the lid.
Alternatively cook on a gentle heat for about 45 minutes to 1 hour until the ginger is tender.
Add the sugar and stir well to dissolve it before simmering for about an hour.
When the ginger is ready, remove jars one by one onto a prepared area, covered to prevent the jars from contacting a cold surface (see notes at the beginning of the chapter on PRESERVING).
Using a funnel and slotted spoon, pack the ginger chunks into the jars and fill up with syrup almost to the top.
Tighten the lids immediately while the contents are still hot. This

will seal the jars if done correctly.

Any surplus syrup can be ladled or poured into the bottles and sealed in the same way.

CANDIED ANGELICA

If you have angelica growing in the garden it's easy to preserve it for cake decorating. It will not have the deep green colour of commercial angelica unless you add green food colouring. (I leave mine natural so can't give a quantity for adding colouring. Follow instructions on the product you use.)

Wash the angelica stems and cut into short lengths.
Cover with water and bring to the boil. Simmer until tender. About an hour.
If using food colouring add at this point. (I leave mine natural so I can't guarantee the process here.)
Add approximately 1 cup of sugar to 1 cup of water, stirring well to dissolve the sugar.
Simmer for 45 minutes. Turn off the heat and allow it to stand for 24 hours.
Repeat the addition of sugar, stirring well and simmering for 30 minutes.
Again, allow it to stand for 24 hours.
Repeat again the next day and the day after (4 days in total).
Allow to cool completely then remove the angelica from the syrup and dry on a silicone mat or greaseproof paper.

When the surface is dry, store in a screw top jar. Will keep for 2 years.

Use the left-over syrup to stew sour fruit such as under-ripe plums or nectarines.

PARSNIP WINE

Gather all necessary equipment: wine bucket, a long-handled spoon and a two litre plastic bottle with the top cut off. Sterilise these with a proprietary wine steriliser. It's essential to maintain strict hygiene or your wine might not work properly. Also essential to rinse away the steriliser before using your equipment. I stand the spoon in a sterilising solution in a plastic water bottle with the top cut off. You will also need a large saucepan or stockpot.
Stay with me - it's much simpler than it sounds!

2kg Parsnips
1 Orange, sliced thinly
1 Lemon, sliced thinly
1 and a half kg Sugar
Packet of wine yeast (Hock is good) or a full teaspoon of all-purpose wine yeast

Wash peel and cut up parsnips into chunks. In a large pan bring them to a boil, then turn heat down and simmer them for 10-15 minutes. No longer or it may cloud the wine.
Allow to cool a little then pour the juice into a sterilised wine bucket. Keep the parsnips and freeze them in containers to add to soups etc. They retain their flavour surprisingly well.
Add the sugar and stir to dissolve.
Top up with cold water to slightly more than the gallon mark on the bucket.
Carefully wash the citrus fruit and slice, being careful not to waste juice. Put slices and any surplus juice into the bucket.
Check with a clean finger that it is no more than blood heat, then put in the yeast and stir gently.
Put the lid on tightly and leave in a warm place for a week to ten days, stirring once a day with the sterilised spoon. You don't need to use new steriliser each day. Just keep the spoon in the sterilising solution in the plastic bottle somewhere convenient and rinse it before and after use.

After a few hours you will hear it start bubbling. A lovely, satisfying sound. The lid will also feel tight as the gas from the yeast pushes against it. Good signs that your yeast is active.

At the end of the week you will need a demijohn, a straining bag (clean, sterilised tights will do), a good -sized funnel and an airlock inserted in a bung.

Sterilise all the equipment.

Stand the rinsed demijohn in the sink with the funnel inserted in the neck. Place the straining bag over the funnel.
Pour the liquid carefully into the demijohn through the funnel. The bucket will be heavy. If you can't manage to tip it safely, sterilise a ladle and use that.
Leave a gap at the neck of the demijohn to take the bung. Put water into the airlock and put the top on. Press the bung in tightly to exclude air. Pretty soon you will see bubbles rising and escaping through the airlock.
Leave in a warm spot for a couple of weeks or more until the airlock has stopped bubbling. Check carefully that you can't see any small bubbles rising in the wine.

Now for the tricky bit. You will need a clean, sterilised demijohn, a funnel, a solid bung and a long tube (preferably with an attachment that sits in the neck of the demijohn.

You can buy them from wine suppliers or a department store's wine-making section.) I also have a stand which holds the demijohn at an angle but you can manage without it with a bit of care.

Place the full demijohn of fermented wine on the work-surface or a table. Do this as gently as possible so you don't stir up the yeast.
Put the clean empty one on the floor with the funnel in the neck. Then put the tube into the wine but keep it above the yeast. (Easier if you have the attachment I mentioned above.)
Suck on the tube until you feel the wine hit your mouth. Quickly place your finger over the end to stop the flow. Let the tube hang

down into the funnel and remove your finger. The wine will run into the demijohn below.

Keep an eye on it so you don't stir up the yeast. When you've drawn off the wine to the level of the yeast, quickly remove the tube from your original demijohn to stop the flow.

There will probably be a gap at the top of the jar. Add cold water but leave room in the neck for the bung. Now firmly push in the sterilised bung (helps to dry it first on a clean piece of kitchen paper) and leave the wine in a cool dark place to mature. Some winemakers leave it for a year but a few weeks is sufficient.

It's a good idea to cover the bung with a cloth tied with a rubber band to keep out dust if the bung should work loose. Check occasionally to make sure it's still tightly enclosed.

Never add any chemicals to clear the wine. If you have made it properly it will clear naturally and produce a beautiful, golden wine. I have done it this way successfully for years.

Save some wine bottles for when you want to bottle your wine but don't ever use screw caps as these could explode if the wine begins to ferment again in storage.

When you're ready to bottle the wine you will need: the length of tube again, funnel, 6 wine bottles, 6 corks and a corking tool.

It's a big help if you have a little tap attached to the end of your tube. These can be bought from wine-making shops or online.

Sterilise all the equipment except the corking tool and rinse well. Paper towels are handy in case of spills. Never, ever, use a screw top on your wine bottles. Home-made wine can start fermenting again and the bottles would explode!! Corks will be forced out so you could lose some wine but no harm done. Never had a problem over 30 years.

Place your demijohn carefully on the worktop. Try not to disturb any sediment.

It helps to put some newspaper on the floor as it gets a bit drippy.

Stand a bottle on the floor (if your tube isn't long enough, stand the bottle on a stool or chair. This is what I do.) You need to have the bottle lower than the demijohn so the wine will flow down into it.

Place the funnel in the neck of the bottle. Place the tube in the wine and suck until the wine flows. Place your finger over the end or turn the little tap to stop the flow.

Place the end of the tube into the funnel and allow the wine to flow into the bottle. Fill to just above the shoulder of the bottle. Leave room for your cork.

If you haven't got a tap on the tube you will need some-one else to remove the bottle and place another ready for filling. Much easier if you have a tap.

Then place a cork into the corking tool (flogger) and push the cork into the neck of the bottle. I find a hammer helps here to force the tool to push the cork in.

Leave the bottles at room temperature to dry off overnight, then label them and store in a dark cool place until you use them.

ABOUT THE AUTHOR

Freda Maxfield

I've been fortunate to share a varied, exciting life for over fifty years with my husband, Allan, and our son and daughter. I married at seventeen, lived in Canada in the 60s and 70s, gained a BA in Humanities, followed by an MLitt as a mature student and retired some years ago from my university research post.

I've always been a creative person who loves to paint, write poetry, sew, knit, crochet and cook. I am also a keen gardener with over fifty years experience of growing fruit, vegetables and flowers. After my daughter encouraged me to write about these activities I started a blog called Earthy Homemaker to celebrate the joy of simple creative pleasures at home through recipes, paintings, garden photography and poetry. When readers started to request a compilation of my recipes I decided to write my own cookbook. It has been such a pleasure to write and illustrate, and a privilege to share my ideas with others.

Review Request
Thank you for reading Earthy Homemaker's Cookbook. If you en-

joyed this book (or even if you didn't) please visit the site where you purchased it and write a brief review. Your feedback is important to me and will help other readers decide whether to read the book too.

Printed in Dunstable, United Kingdom